IN THE ME

This book is to be returned on or before
the last date stamped below.

angus

district

libraries

*also by Elizabeth Jennings
from Carcanet*

Collected Poems
Selected Poems
Tributes
Times and Seasons
Familiar Spirits

The Sonnets of Michelangelo
(translations)

Every Changing Shape
(essays)

IN THE MEANTIME

Elizabeth Jennings

CARCANET

First published in 1996 by
Carcanet Press Limited
402-406 Corn Exchange Buildings
Manchester M4 3BY

A CIP catalogue record for this book
is available from the British Library
ISBN 1 85754 256 8

The publisher acknowledges financial assistance
from the Arts Council of England

Set in 10 pt Palatino by Bryan Williamson, Frome
Printed and bound in England by SRP Ltd, Exeter

For Priscilla

Contents

The Right Givers

Give me the honest benefactors who
    Do not offer gifts
Out of duty but who clearly show
It delights them. How the darkness lifts

From my own sky when such guide me towards
    Wild gardens where I can
Wander. Do not traffic with rewards
Or make me some rich prize but rather, then,

Invite me to take part in an event,
    A music-party, say,
Of amateurs whose every instrument
Is gracious, equal too. And so, I pray,

If you are giving for reward elsewhere,
    Do not come to me,
But if you're gentle, show me that you share
Some need also and then your gift will be

Carefully chosen, not too large but full
    Of some lack that you have
Which I can help to heal and make you whole,
Like shyness, dark moods, even lack of love.

Prawning

We went along because we trusted him,
Our grandfather, my mother's father who
Taught us darts, setting us near the board.
And then his tall and steady strides were in
The rockpools, and he didn't seem to need
His eyes. Something instinctive as the wind
Guided his tough net under every fringe
Of slimy seaweed. Almost at his beck
It seemed, the prawns fell in his net, a dozen
Or even more at one good push and pull,
We copied him, my sister and myself,
Aped his wait and thrust, but ours were quick,
Too quick and awkward. We were smelling salt
And iodine within North Devon tide-out.
We raced along, sometimes sliding, sometimes
Slipping a moment in the green and laughing,
Then off we went. The birds were circling high,
The sea was far-away, would not encroach
For several hours.
                              So many times we went
Prawning with Grandpa Turner and we loved
The craft we tried to copy, healthy breeze,
Feeling of being well yet all these came
Together in a mood of love and trust.
He must have caught nearly a pound each time
He took us prawning. Grandpa Turner was
A skilled, fresh-water angler too. He'd stand
Flicking his bait and seem to wait for ever.
These untimed events we treasure later,
Come upon them as we fall asleep.
Nothing mystical, nothing holy
Except that such a craft enjoyed with children
Is precious always. Prawns were flung in water
Piping hot, soon dead. We had no qualms
About their deaths. In Nature's hierarchies
They fitted in a happy part of childhood,
The age of ten's a treasured time for me,
I could not see the clouds ahead, the turning
Inward for years. I shut my eyes and summon

A Devon of the heart's imagination,
All seas out far, high birds with lofty music
When Grandpa Turner caught our bumper supper.

Wisdom of the Fields

It's all built up, with ugly houses too,
That stretch of far North Oxford where my father
Bought a house. He told us with a glow,
'No rents for us. This house is strong, will weather

And rise in price.' Behind us was a field
And all through Summer (surely sun shone then
Every afternoon) we shoved and pulled
At fences to get in and always when

The hay was thigh-high, we would gather piles
So that the quick hands of my sister could
Weave the hay between bent willows. Smells
Inside these Summer igloos were of wood

And something very old we had no name for.
Small houses stand there now, two cars apiece.
Where are the children who should be out there?
Our counterparts, our ghosts? No sign of these,

Most likely they're in Greece or Tenerife,
Names we had never heard of but I swear
We learnt a wisdom in our playing life
That can't be found on hot sand anywhere.

Spring Love

I must accept that love will never come
As it did once – quickly and unexpected
Casting a radiance on any room

That I worked in – I could be unprotected
Because surprise was the chief element
Of love like this only at me directed

And coming to me like a sacrament
Unearned and hard to credit. Part of this
Was that for years I thought that love was meant

For other people, that it would not bless
And cherish me. I was the second child,
Awkward, competitive and thinking less

Of everything would come to me. A wild
Creature I was, searching for meaning in
The universe. I never could be mild

Or sure. I never guessed love would begin
Romantically. I was caught up in it,
Amazed, enthralled and wholly altered when

I was first kissed with passion. Now I sit
Watching Spring suggest itself. There's pain
In thinking of dead loved ones yet – O yet

I feel my blood race in my veins again
And words unfolding with the leaves while birds
Call tentatively. Poems I knew sustain

Me as love did at first. There's a refrain
Singing within me, finding me fresh words.

The Liberation

It happened one day
It really did ·
I was off to school
But a new one now
The classroom was bright
The mistress was kind
She smiled as she taught
O and suddenly, wonderfully
I understood
The meaning of words
I wrote an essay
Recited poems
And I was freed
From the bars of my cage
For ever and ever
And now I was bold
Would enjoy the games
Even more than work
In this golden world
I was any age
I could touch the stars
I was ten years old.

Dream

A dream without a nightmare element,
What leaning into light, what gracious chance.
Even the strangers with kind gestures lent
Towards but not inside our ring of dance.

There was an easy grandeur which I could
Lose myself in and never feel the shy
Child I once was when a party mood
Was always dark though I could not say why.

One presence oversaw and yet took part
For suddenly I felt his arm around
My waist, and dances beating in my heart.

Music we moved to had a well-known sound
And yet I did not have to name its art
But only knew we moved on holy ground.

Their First Snow

This is the first time they have seen it and
At first it looks like icing on a cake.
They wrap up well and try to understand
How they can use it for they want to make
A house, a man, or anything that comes
To mind. Their muffled hands will pick it up
Roll it round and throw it till it homes
Upon a wall, a roof or it falls deep
And soundlessly. They've found a silent world
For the first time and now they like it so
But soon, in spite of running, they are cold.
Their hands are hurting and they all run through
Entries to home, no longer swift and bold
But slow and burning. Some are crying too.

A House in Nottingham

Everything I hear is beautiful,
    Everything I see
Blends and attends. Here I've come to feel
A care where only suffering can be

The chosen and the decorator. Each
    Room has thick, soft mats
And there are enormous windows. Light can reach
You easily. There are no noisy pets

Because a little girl has Down's Syndrome.
    How may hours were spent
In teaching her to read and write? Quick fear
    Is present that she may
Fall or be frightened. Yes, it's always her
Spirit and flesh which weigh here night and day.

But she gives back untarnished love, whole trust
    Even to strangers. In
A world like ours of hourly crime she must
Be guarded. She's not capable of sin

And both her parents guard her innocence
    Gladly and with awe,
But suffering took them long ago. You sense
It in the calm, but when her parents saw

They had a Mongol baby they must have
    Been shocked. They hint they were.
But their child has evoked enduring love.
The doors close softly. There is much light here.

For Charlotte

with Down's Syndrome

We are shallow if we say that you
Need our pity since you have a lack.
There are many things that you can do
Much as we can. You can read and make
Pretty things. You show

Skill though it is hard for you to learn.
You teach us patience, yes, but so much more,
You keep an eye on us and you discern
Our many moods. In your life there's a pure
Vision you must earn

By slowness for you have no knowledge of
Facile thinking, acting. In our world
You show immediate feeling, gentle love
But you are at the mercy of our cold
Moments and must move

With hard precision. Everything is fraught
With risk for you. You run to hug us and
Never doubt that we shall understand
And give love back to you. You've never thought
If we should take your hand

Gently and repay your total trust.
Today I met you and tonight I can't
Forget what you are teaching. You are just
Where we take easy sides. How much I want
You now when I am lost.

Yes, lost by cruelty where I must live,
Planned animosity. I find you where
Kindness is all about. Your parents give
Me gracious love to which you add your care
And start to heal my grief.

Children in Summer

We sweat and grumble and the noon sun has
No mercy on us. Tiny gusts of breeze
Blow through one block of flats and its close neighbour.
'This is the Tropics' murmurs someone. Here
Is an old city loved, throughout all Europe.
Tension is felt. Too many tourists press
Their way on narrow streets, too many tongues
Shout gibberish. The streets are filthy with
Countless black spots made by alfresco eating,
But one thing can't be missed.
Children cavort and leap about. Their spindly
Legs are dressed in highly-coloured tights,
They wear the rainbow like a true parade
Of little models. Most of all they have not
Lost their zest for heat and sun that's strewn
Everywhere. Our trees are drying up.
And soon – and this is August still – they will
Lose their leaves to clothe our streets. I think
That Summer is a mood to perfect childhood.
Strawberries are still about and orange lollies
Please the avaricious tongues of children.
They are the planets' keepers. Let them be
Proud and cool, impatient with all who
Curse as another camera snaps a view.

Child of Seven Questions

In Chechnya

What are they doing? How are they thinking? Why
    Does nobody smile at me?
I can see that everyone's staring up at the sky
As if they were tied to the ground. They are not free

As my friends and I were before this happening
    Upon such a usual day.
Now we can feel our own eyes opening
Wide and our game is over. We cannot say

Anything now but why and what and how.
    Helpless our elders seem.
Time touches us in a panic-stricken Now.
We imagine in play. Is this a grown-up dream

And have they somehow painted the clouds all black
    And why do their fingers shake?
O I think that we are learning the lesson of lack
And the world like our games is now beginning to break.

The Need to Praise

What do you say when Summer returns overnight,
When the world is painted in deep, rich gold? You want
New words for sudden Summer.
After cold nights and icy mornings, we were
Bathed in sunshine and felt lighter wherever
We went and however long
We stayed. I am a Summer child whose birthday
Is in July but here was Summer all over
Again, all over the late grass of our meadows
And the half-dome of the sky was a radiant blue.
I wanted to praise, I needed a new *Book of Hours*
Painted by unseen holy ones, enchanted
By God as man and creator of the world.
O it is sweet to be
Suddenly warm in October in suddenly green
Fields and ubiquitous trees.

Oxford, Heatwave, Tourists

Lift up your eyes, I say,
Above the upper windows of tall houses,
Above the horror of high-rise grey, stone flats,
Above the dirty air and all the pallid pollutions.
Lift up your eyes
A foot or a yard or so.

Because in this city tight-packed, angry with tourists
The dwellers here feel cast out,
Yes, I feel cast out,
In this attention to a pleasure of helpful breeze
I gazed a yard or two above some roof-tops
Of beauty and colleges, squares and orchards and gardens,
I lifted my eyes up to the limpid sky
And found examples of very strange architecture,
Churches and mosques and ladders assertively leading
Up to alleged Heaven.
And as I sat on a low wall
I felt another, almost-ghost of a city
Try to gain my attention and when it did
I found a purity, a vernal perfection
About attic windows not seen
On ordinary days.
There was a sense of beauty beyond beauty
As the day distributed its dusty moments
Among a rain-wanting sky.

So I say look up only a few rungs
Of imagination's ladder
And you will find a city inviting you
To hear all its bells and enter.

Somerset

Such gentle open slopes, such lack of drama.
A cottage there and there a tiny town
lodged in a valley, rivers overflowing
after four rainy months
but all is drying now as ubiquitous sun
points out a church spire then a gaze of windows
an almost temperate time but not quite yet.
Who knows what March may bring? Perhaps some snow
but for this Sunday late in February
Spring slips its head round corners of big clouds
and they are silvered by the raptured sun
and by me gazing. Here all good that's England
speaks in green flows of light, in church-bells ringing
while afternoons are stretching out their arms
before the good day of our clocks put forward.

Among Late-Teenagers

You wait in a half-circle, serious eyes
Upon me as I enter. Do you see
My nervous fingers? I begin to read
Sitting. I don't stand. This is a class
Because you have to read my poetry
For your A Levels. Do you notice me
Stopping briefly as my fingers pass

Over the pages? Now and then I pause
While you ask wise and tactful questions. I
Try to answer, telling you about
How I write. 'Do poems come easily?'
'Do form and subject come quite separately
Or both at once?' More probing, 'Tell us why
You write in verse, not prose.' Always I try

To answer simply though part of my mind
Reflects, 'At your age I was reading Keats,
Not someone living.' Then I read more poems
Which do not feel like any part of me.
Next I tell you there's much luck for poets
Using the English tongue. Now the talk gets
More personal but in a kindly way.

I'm thinking what a world we've made for you.
Your love of poems will not earn you a living,
And then – no nonsense here – our spirits seem
To meet and I am learning something of
Your quick responsibility, your giving
So much to me now that is part of love.

Welcoming Spring

Give me new words for Spring. There must be some.
Delight wells up in me. I'm almost drunk
To see the daffodil and crocus bloom
And a huge cloudless sky. Winter has slunk

Away, a guilty thing that is ashamed
It came among us darkening each good mood.
We let it go like a small pang we dreamed
Now all we see and smell is ardent, good.

And I mean good in every kind of sense –
Sweet, desirable, in morals, right.
Who can be angry when such wreaths of scent

Sweeten our noses? Such a rainbow sight
Stands everywhere in its own circumstance,
What seer's know now ours in shafts of light.

The Great Spirits

The trouble is we are all loose and mixed,
    A shape of mind and then
The body slow and wanting to be fixed
Somewhere, and all bear witness to this when

They fall in love. Why fall? It seems to raise
    Us to the sky, to hills?
Love is the power within us when we praise
Each other. Nature, works of art. It kills

The half-achieved, the tepid thought, the wish
    Half-realised. Have you
Met anyone whose spirit shone through flesh?
I have myself encountered one or two,

And loved their modest power, their gentle worth,
    Their give-and-seldom-take,
O these are gods who rise above the earth.
Trying to reach them mostly means heartbreak.

Story Tellers

The tellers of tales give more than reading a book
They make things up as they go along, they will add
     And annotate and digress. They don't mind being interrupted
And corrected. Children gather round them in rapture
     And this is the start of history when history meets
Imagination. Imagination will always walk off
     With the golden trophies, the prizes, the best
Their listeners can afford. I'm about to visit just now
     A narrator I know who tells tall stories and short ones.
I await his latest and I'm on my way to get it.
     You can race me if you like but you won't overtake me
And I won't tell any more.

Seers and Makers

There is one quality in common which
    Artists and men of prayer
Display when we think back on them. They were
    Eager to disappear
Within the words, paint, sound, and praying; each
Wished to be hidden. Thus we can
Always mark off the honest from the sham.

The artist and the holy man also
    Always share energy.
When a saint prays you see his goodness grow
    His rapture you can see
In his concentration. Great art shows
Impatient feeling. Mind and sense debate.
Will is at work and there's no touch of fate,

Self disappears when man becomes his prayer,
    Likewise man and his art,
And both aim at perfection and will share
    Any wound or hurt.
But seers accept while artists cannot bear
To leave their work untouched. Some detail's wrong
In poems, buildings or a catch of song.

Hermits and Poets

Do they move with empty minds so that
Meditation may have room enough?
Or are they filled with this world's appetites
Which must be cleared out by a perfect love?

A love few of us know or want to learn,
It is so dark. In deserts or at night
The spirit of an eremite must burn
With God's own hardly bearable good light.

Imagination shaping poems can seem
The purest moments of one's life and yet
We know, when coming from that trance, a dream
Was working in us and the poem is set

Down and finished, such experience
May seem at times like perfect meditation
But words or images are what enchants,
What seemed like prayer was only concentration.

But all poets know that their best work is given
So they should not be thanked and they know too
That if a few lines hold a hint of Heaven
It can't be forced if ever it rings true.

We don't deserve it when somebody writes
Or says a verse of ours has helped so much,
We are surprised, for when a poem delights
Some power has given it a magic touch.

The Sitter

O for the selflessness a painter has
    When he paints nakedness
With lack of lust even if hands may pass
Over a woman's flesh to put her as

His picture needs. At any age the rest
    Of us can't help but feel
A touch of some desire, a hint of lust
And wish that we could watch as painters will

And children too but surely no one else.
    The petty nastiness
Is that our own desires are also false
For we mind, when we're old, if lust grows less.

Innocence is afar in every way,
    In childhood and in myth.
We are deceived when wishing we could say
We own pure looks for eyes to wander with.

Act of the Imagination

Surely an Act of the Imagination
    Helps more than one of Faith
When a doubt brushes us. We need strong passion
To summon miracles. Life after death,

Bread turning into flesh and blood from wine,
    I need to cast around
And find an image for the most divine
Concepts. My mind must move on holy ground,

And then the hardest creed – the rising from
    Death when Christ indeed
Bled finally – ideas cannot come
As barren notions. Yes, I always need

Herbert's sonnet 'Prayer' say, or that great
    Giotto painting for
My heart to leap to God. I want to meet
Him in my own poems, God as metaphor

And rising up. I watch a lucid sky
    And see a silver cloud
And Christ's behind it; this is part of faith,
Hear the Great Hours sung and let faith be loud

With the best imagining we have.
    This is how I approach
My God-made-Man. Thus I learn to love
And yes, like Thomas, know Christ through a touch.

For Paul Klee

Such a fastidious colourist, this man,
    The painter who truly knew
School or movement. All his work began
And ended where imagination's glow

Enchanted everything. Klee's was a world
    Wholly fastidious.
And it is out of time and always bold.
The painter's character is given to us

Unsparingly. Klee's world is never one
    Which he hides in. It is
Shaped without mirrors. Everything is done
To show a place open to everyone.

A painter of quick patterns, colourist
    Whose palette knows no lack
Or so it seems. Here is an art of rest,
And of sophistication. Klee gives back

Ideas of worlds where artists did not sign
    Their pictures, let them go
As gifts to anyone. Klee's touch and line
Show us the bounds and make sure that we know

The rules of art. Surrendering is one.
    A brush can be a wand
Which can be potent even over sun
And, like a prayer, can reach beyond beyond.

Order

We shape, we cut, we steal, we wrap, we are
Makers of order where there wasn't one.
Think of our topiary when all trees wear
The same, shaped, scissored look. Yes, we have done

This to most wildernesses. After we
Were driven from that garden, we've shown how
There must be patterns. We lost liberty
Of one kind but we've fashioned others. Now

In our wild world of misrule we insist
On shapeliness and balance. Most of us
Do this to gardens. Tough weeds will persist

Until we've plucked them. We make curious
Designs for garden-beds. O we exist
To make new order since our Eden loss.

Sonnets to Narcissus

I

Homage is due to you because you show
In a myth's magic way a reason to
Value the mirror and all it can show,
O but what danger lies in this also.

But isn't every work of art a kind
Of play with the reflection and the glass?
We think that in a glance we read a mind
And lovers always long to read a face.

The peril here is obvious and sweet,
A true temptation but a gracious one.
Sometimes in mirrors two loved faces meet

And here love starts its glimpse from one to one
And looking-glances show we can repeat
And thus right love is carefully made complete.

II

Imagine worlds without some form of mirror.
We cannot make this act at all because
Men first gazed into streams. Did they feel terror,
Seeing themselves repeated there or was

It a delight to learn their eyes, their hair,
Their noses, cheeks? Of course such men
Did not know it was themselves they saw
But there our inward-looking ways began.

Was this the death of innocence, this knowing
Yourself so soon by heart? Did selfishness
Start here, and pride, in this so shining showing?

Perhaps. It makes good sense. Such happiness
We gain indeed when our own selves start going
Outward. Be wise and break the looking-glass.

III

Holy ones have always sought to find
A place of silence where no noise intrudes.
They search beyond themselves, their heart and mind
To be united with a living God.

Satan, of course, always sought them out
Would turn them inward to themselves alone
And there they were besieged by clever doubt
And voices which would break the calmest souls.

Many would then reflect upon their Lord
Who prayed within a garden to find there
Moments that aren't conjured by a word.

For Christ was tempted and into his prayer
Came all the world's proud voices doubting God,
Whilst damaged peace was obvious everywhere.

Having it Both Ways

What liberty we have when out of love,
Our heart's back in its place, our nerves unstrung,
Time cannot tease us, and once more we move
In step with it. Out of love we're strong,

Without its yearnings and the way it makes
All virtues vices. Steady liberty
Is our element and no heartbreaks
Can touch or take us. We are nobly free.

But how long can we live within this state?
Don't we miss the slow encroachment of
Possessive passion? Don't we half-await

Its cruel enchantments which no longer have
Power over us? O we are obdurate,
Begging for freedom, hankering for love.

Touch

Touch. How much it starts and how much ends.
Each sacrament demands it and all love,
Whether of passion or the play of friends,

Asks for its use. God started this world of
Shape and substance. The whole universe
Stirred by his touching it at every move.

Eden – the potent tale of our reverse,
Was darkened by the picking of a fruit
When touch was disobedient. Its curse

Spoilt touch and yet it also somehow brought
God-Man to us and put him at our will.
Touch can demonstrate an arcane thought

And love surrenders when its power goes still.

Telling the Time

Telling the time has little to do with hours
    Or seconds, minutes, day.
Time is one of the spirit's inimical powers
    And you learn it in the way

You fall in love with someone who doesn't care
    For any part of you.
At best, it whispers through an ardent prayer
    But time has more to do

With any happy friendship and it has
    Full power over love.
It makes you think of how all good must pass.
    Yes, it's the enemy of

Falling in love. It makes you fall indeed.
    It tells you expertly
That no love lasts though what does last is need,
    And time stalks liberty.

It makes us fear an end before it comes
    And haunts all sweet farewells,
It is the dark dissembler of our dreams
    And it can leap from bells

Which enter marriages just as they start.
    You cannot hold time back.
It dizzies every movement of the heart
    And is in love with lack.

Two Sonnets

for my mother who has been dead for two years

I

Your natural wisdom is what I remember,
Your clever hands re-shaping, sewing, cooking.
You always come back to me in September
When St Giles' fair still is making
Its noise in roundabouts and in loud colour,
Straight to the bull your dart went but you said,
'It was a fluke.' All pleasures you made fuller
And gave them back from heart as much as head.
Nothing you did was vulgar or a fluke,
You had an instinct about poetry
For making was your life. You loved a book
By Jane Austen or Trollope. You could see
The point of writing poems and you took
My first ones to the post. You are with me

II

Not as sadness but a presence who
Shaped my life. So often I was ill
And once you kept the fire up all night through,
And in the morning you were with me still.
You never chided my dull awkwardness,
Falling, slipping, breaking. You could see
My skill and elegance in writing this
Or that small verse. I owe you poetry
For I've no doubt your making gift became
Mine in another way. You were so proud
Of my first books and loved to see my name
Upon the spines. I hear you read aloud
Often in the night still for you were
Gentle, strong and quick, beyond the crowd.

A World of Love

Since early childhood I have been in love
Or loved or looked up to from far, someone.
My early childhood passions meant far-off
Gazing at. I've always seen a sun

In my half-real and half-imagined world.
What good pours through all children when they can
Almost worship, copy. There's no cold
Climate in my country. I can scan

And stare at stars, and often I have read
The words of seers, tried to understand
How they are lost in God. There is no dead

Place for me. I have a pulsing land
Peopled with saints and children. These I need
To help me see in joy and pain, God's hand.

Loss of Loss

It never brings relief that we can wake
    Up without a fear
Of some cruel loss, a heart- or a death-break,
I think of this just now when I am clear

Of all the guilt and horror your death brought.
    I hid away to grieve,
People shunned me. Grief, it seems, is caught,
A sickness that can feed on happy life.

Now I wake up and do not think of how
    You've gone away for good
And yet there is a vacuum in me now,
I mourn because I can't mourn as I should.

How shallow we all are, we never can
    Be sure of what we'll feel,
Except we learn a power that's greater than
We ever guessed and nobody can heal.

At Mass (I)

Why are we not amazed? How can we kneel
    And stare or else, perhaps,
Find our minds wandering? We ought to feel
Awestruck. A bell is rung and the bread wraps

Christ thinly in it. This is for our sake
    Lest we should feel afraid.
The wine's for drinking and the priest will break
The bread as on that night when Jesus laid

His life down for us. Did they understand,
    His chosen, what it meant
To bring God into bread? A human hand
Takes gently what is kind and heaven-sent.

The drama is tomorrow. History has
    A place for crucified
God-made-man to teach us to learn peace.
It was for this that Christ bore pain and died.

All he had promised came about. He knew
    Peter would deny
His lord and master. So do we also.
The Mass is gentle, prayer is but a sigh.

And yet, and yet... at times most of us hope
    That all the world will see
The magnitude, yes, the enormous scope
Of what the Mass means so that all may be

Sorry and say so, mourn and maybe cry,
    For all creation here
Has waited for God-man to testify
That he can conquer every kind of fear.

But we are wrong. All that our saviour did
    Depended on free-will.
Time ceases when the gold ciborium's lid
Is lifted and Christ comes to us as still

As he was at his birth. Now death and birth
    Are changed that we may live,
Yes, live abundantly and by our Faith
Accept what all the Godhead longed to give.

Which is Which?

I'm vexed with this delight
Because I cannot say what spirit is
And what mere flesh. I'm driven by the light
And only want to clap my hands and praise.

Spirit, they say, works through
Our feeble senses and transfigures them,
But my five senses through all rapture go
And yet I know my spirit has to come

Into all this someway
Because what I am feeling at this hour
Is what I rarely feel when I can pray.
Which is the stronger, soul or body's power?

After Dark

How will it be when we're fleshless?
What shall we do?
Will our minds climb invisible stairs
So that we too
Reach the moon or see a new star?
I do not know.

I only know that when I shut
My eyes I sometimes can
Re-invent the world to my own plan
Which can seem so much heaven
That I now stare at sun or the moon
And feel part of limited men

When Lazarus rose from his tomb.
Why did his friends not ask
What it felt like to be dead?
Was it too hard to ask?
No harder to credit than
The Godhead in a white disc?

I close my eyes and my usual world escapes
And I throw off time like a coat.
I seem to be spirit entirely.
I move where I wish.
I am my own story and plot
But time turns me back in to flesh,
Flesh and the spirit of thought.

At Mass (II)

It is so simple and so quiet that we
Gather round and make small bows and look
At all the others present. Gradually
The celebration works on us.
A book tells us how to be

A part of all the wonder happening
And soon enough we realise the awe
We ought to feel. Here God is opening
His secrets. Human law

Is broken and a great event occurs,
Hidden, yes, but only that we may
Not be afraid. The wine a server pours
Becomes Christ's blood, the same as on the day
He died upon the cross.

This great occasion started long ago
In an Upper Room. Here Christ's own blood
Is present once again. The priest will show
The Little Round to be our daily food,
We pause in what we do,

Every day. Our marvelling to prayer
Nothing matters but this Holy Meal,
The angels bow and time can disappear
As we gaze and simply want to kneel
To show our faith. We're near

Eternity and every bad thing done
By us we're sorry for. Our hearts are made
Bethlehems for God the Father's son
Who is God and wants us unafraid
And only see what's true.

Every moment of enchantment we've
Ever known joy here is present and
Our best love is shown when we receive
God so simply. We can understand
Less than we believe.

For here all intuitions gather to
Show our hopes are valid and made clear.
Passion falters. Love alone will do
As God shows his creation need not fear
Great wishes won't come true.

The rite proceeds. The world comes spinning back
And we return to find all usual things
Are shining with right purpose.
                              What seemed luck
Is given while our hurt creation sings
And there is no more lack.

Bread

What ashes and what sackcloth now?
    We more than eat our fill each day.
Lent is upon us. Few think how
    To do some penance and still see
    Christ's agony.

He is with us in the Bread
    That's consecrated everywhere,
And still a few take on a need
    And show their sorrow in a prayer
    And so repair

Their own and others' faults. They feel
    All of Christ's suffering is still
About and some try how to heal
    And help his steps up on that hill
    Where men could kill

God as man. This mystery
    Wise men could never understand
But here and there in history
    A seer comes to comprehend
    A Man-God's end.

O yes he died. The sky went black,
    Christ's own disciples fled away
Like Peter who would mourn his lack.
    Our world is black and still we slay
    Our God each day.

Consecration (I)

It all happens so slowly. A few words
Are spoken. Such tiny words
Full of more than this world can ever contain
In its random occasions, its pell-mell actions which we
Have brought about. It is to change what we see
And hear all about us that this Round of bread
Is changed, becomes Christ's life on earth when he
Chose to move among us all, to free
Our trammelled spirits. He loves liberty
So he became for a time what all of us are
All the time. His words go on echoing where
Any will listen. One simple breath of prayer
Will break our chains, abandon our daily fear.
For this he arrived and stays on our desperate star.

Consecration (II)

'This is . . .' The priest lifts up
The Round of Bread and we
Wait for the risen cup.
So that no ecstasy

Should too excite us, God
Hides in this frail Host
And then we drink his Blood,
Wine to us. Our dust

Through all the ages has
Brought us to this event.
In any simple Mass,
Christ is so quietly lent

To all. We fold our hands
And try to pray. Who can
Find words? Mass starts and ends
With hiding God-made-Man.

Ash Wednesday 1995

This moment is tremendous yet is veiled
    In a thin Round of bread.
We must use our imaginations which have failed
So often to help us towards the truth. Instead

We have let them lean toward violence
    Where not one thing is safe.
Nature may move in her ancient, timeless dance
But we have let go and we swing off

Hither and thither, untrusting, loveless, caught
    In a murderous mood we invade.
Let me on this Ash Wednesday create a thought
That is open and innocent, something which I have made

But more a way of being that I have been given,
    A chance to make a choice,
After six weeks of Lent may I be shriven
And echo from my distance Christ's dying voice.

A Touch of Existentialism

How essence and existence fascinate.
The soul's born with us. When we start to grow
Existence takes us over and we start,
Given free-will, to be, to learn, to know.

Firstly it seems to grow like monkeys who
Ape our actions. Then we seem obscure
Within ourselves but outwardly also.
But soon we marvel that we own a pure

Faculty for feeling stars like powers
To know bravado, while imagination
Guides us among the fleet, assertive flowers.

But we were meant for more than this. A passion
Teaches us ecstasy and how to pause
Within our central place in all creation.

Holy Communion

There were some miracles intended to
Save us from too much awe and wonderment.
How simple are the things a priest must do
To close Christ in a simple element.
The Round of Bread is so

Tiny, thin and white. It almost makes
Us feel we must protect the Godhead when
The Host looks like what any woman bakes
For her small family. The wisest man
Says nothing when he takes

The little wafer. What can any word
Explain of this kind, gentle element?
Silence is the way God is adored.
Vaster than galaxies, this sacrament
Holds Bethlehem's young Lord.

The Spirit's Power

All the sheen and cut, the tied, the true
Of almost anything I praise and watch.
I clap my hands when Nature shows her due
Respect for us but how does spirit go

On? Strip off each trying sense, think how
The spirit works. It has its own success
As I think hard and leave the here and now.
My spirit is the way that I seek grace

And how it corresponds with what I do.
The flesh creeps slowly offering dubious powers.
I will five senses off but they won't go

For long, I have known rare and kindly hours
That leap from love and then I think of you
As I last saw you, gathering wild flowers.

Rome

I.

I think I found a counterpart of it,
The balance of the spirit and the flesh,
Forty years ago when Rome was lit
Up night and day as if by my own wish.

I mutely prayed and when the sun came out
For April Easter, Faith was all around
In voice and face and works of art. No doubt
Could last there long. All seemed like holy ground

And so it was. The sun stretched wide and far
And I was touched by it. My spirit knew
The world was worth the saving. I was near

Quick absolution, happiness with true
Purpose. Resurrection was so sure
And oddly this was old and very new.

II.

There was St Peter's and within the great
Sistine Chapel roof was painted, how
God created Adam. With much sweat
Michelangelo made all things Now

And showed how gift and instinct, flesh and soul
Can work as one. How fortunate I was
To see and feel all this and be made whole
As loving care shone out of every face.

Much has gone wrong since almost everywhere
But hope's a beacon in the moon. Each star
Stands over Bethlehem and on us here

For Bethlehem and Resurrection are
Working in each of us. The spirit's clear
And in me I can feel Christ's sweet love stir.

Time's Element

for Robert Ombres O.P.

I know that I was wrong about the hours
    And time and clocks and bells.
I thought that only future had its powers
Upon us. Hearing you, I see the false

Premise and perspective. All that's now
    Indeed is moved into
Futures we can't rely on or know how
Anything that happens there is true.

Of course the past is only sure and feels
    Certain. It is our
History. The future may be false
And any moment take from us one hour.

Then I remembered those prophetic words,
    'Before all was, I am.'
Christ lived among us with a cross and swords
And yet he with his Virgin Mother came

Into the moments of the angels' plea.
    She carried God and man
And gave the future her willed history
As she took part in God the Father's plan.

Calvary

Surely when Christ was hanging on the Cross
He felt all pain, not only that one which
Was obvious to men. I think he was
Suffering all the agonies which touch
Some time each one of us:

The death-camps, torture, hurting thoughts, and all
That claims the flesh and soul of man throughout
History since our chosen lot, the Fall.
Thus God as Man experienced every doubt
And so he had to call

For mercy, yes, God when man could sweat
For all the shame of Peter's cowardice
Though he'd foreknown it. Christ felt every great
And small sin, yet his dying meant success
Though it looked like defeat.

The Assumption of Our Lady 15th August

'Assumed.' What does it mean? Say 'Take for granted'
That is it's workaday, mere connotation.
But take 'Assumption'. It is now enchanted,
Pulsing with life, untainted.

August the 15th will arrive tomorrow
And we shall celebrate the death of one
Who chose to take on every human sorrow.
When she became the mother of God's son.
Mary had to borrow

A stable and a manger where her child
Might sleep and drink her milk. How much did she
Understand? Since she was undefiled,
God's birth came easily.

Yes but from that day on much mystery,
She lost her son when he must go about
His business. But she stood beneath that tree
And understood our doubt.

Yes, this girl accepted everything,
Felt all of grief but never would despair,
She taught the God-man how to walk and sing.
Grace did not save her from man's suffering.
She teaches us to bear

Horror, war, misunderstanding, loss,
She was so young and yet a stoic too.
The sky went dark as she stood by the Cross.
Did she feel triumph too?

Flesh and Spirit

Think flesh away, attempt
    To be pure spirit and
Be in your God so wrapt
    That you can understand

His working and his way
    Of leaving you to let
You find his heart and stay
    In his pure spirit, set

Where time is cast away,
    Where flesh makes no demands
And there's no night or day,
    No limbs, no head, no hands –

But wait, did Christ not come
    To re-perfect our flesh
By making it his home
    And the whole Godhead's wish?

Spirit and Flesh

Although we're chained to flesh and mostly love
Its senses, appetites, the way it gives
Pleasure to us, most of us think of
Another part, the spirit which too lives

And fashions art and our response to art,
Which works through memory and intellect
And sometimes also we speak of the heart
Not meaning that which beats but one which acts

Through judgement, insight... And how often we
Long to lose our bodies and to move
By our imaginations. Liberty

Works here and all the best of human love,
We move beyond the stars and through the sea,
We trust our souls and yet can find no proof.

Lazarus

Why did no one ask you what you saw
    And found when you were dead?
For there's not doubt that dead is what you were.
All breath had gone and you were cold. They laid

You in a tomb and your relations shed
    Tears and mourned for you.
And then, this wonder rising up indeed,
A little Christ. Did no one really know

What to ask? Were they too filled with awe
    And silenced? Or, maybe
All were so joyful at the sight they saw
And so astounded at what they could see

That, at the time at least, no question came
    Into their minds when they
Saw you alive and called you by your name.
It seems more likely that you could not say

What after-death can yield and mean and show,
    That there were no words for
That place or time when human spirits know
This whole vast what? There was no metaphor.

Good Friday

It is the day of death and the burnt-out sun
And the teetering cross and a man who is God crying out
To his hiding Father and he and his Father are one
But the man on the cross carries the world's doubt
And asks where his Father has gone.

So the creed says but today the orderly creed
Is set aside and Man faces God and demands
'I am forsaken by you, and what is the need
I am hanging here and have lost almost all my friends,
And now they loosen my hands.

My mother is here. She holds me again to her breast
But no angel is by, only a frightened few
Who know no reasons but still stay near and trust
They know not what but find there is work to do,
The duties of death now must

Be performed and the mother prays to her son.'
God is brought low and darkness is everywhere,
The bright, unthinking people still look for the sun.
And somewhere the mystery of rising is starting here
Where there is the scent of grass and flowers in the air.
The long hours of Easter Saturday have gone
As the great third Day draws near.

Age of Doubt

Lying on my bed one summer day
I thought of what the Holy Ghost could mean.
Always before I'd taken it on trust
But now it was in doubt. The gold and green

Summer air and grass showed everywhere
But inner dark had taken hold of me.
I thought of mighty birds but now they had
A silly sense. How could a mere bird be

Holy and part of God? It made no sense
And so I started going through my creed,
'God-made-man', 'ascended into Heaven'.
I could not answer and the books I read

Led to more questions. When I asked them, though,
The answers only made me ask afresh,
A fresh new one. I longed so much to know
How God himself could even be 'made flesh'?

Over was all acceptance and glad trust,
And from those days to this I have asked how
Answers can come and fit my magic Creed.
And every dawn I'm more uncertain now.

So maybe just the asking is what God
Seeks out in us and makes our spirits glow.
We want a reason why we should be good.
A God in hiding's all that we can know.

With the Migrants

O let me go with the happy migrants who
Have the accurate instinct when the first cold bites,
Give me their feathers and wings, their joyful trust
As they brim the clouds and veer with the precious blue.
I'll be no hibernator, rather go
To the warmth of the world, the jocund moods of it.
I can almost think myself into a swift's
Slender body. I would keep my hope
And my imagination but coupled with
Their hope and certainty, their joyous lives.
I have seen swifts go and felt a strange nostalgia
As if I once were one of them indeed.
And so, according to many theories, I am.
How tender yet tough their wings look, how they seem
To signal Southward a message from the North.
I close my eyes on this September night
Of sudden cold and I am indeed away
But most of all when I'm on the tip of sleep
I am spreading my wings, I am off with a rightful faith.

In the Meantime

In the meantime. What does it mean?
First of course that there's time further on,
Hour upon hour, second on second
And days and nights. I know I mean
A pause as if
I had plenty of days, volumes of weeks.
But who really knows?
I think I am certain that this is a pause
And later on
Will be just the right time in every sense
For the message I'm sending now, just a message.

I beg you to wait. How can I know
That you have the time and it's worth the wait?
It sounds like arrogance and presumption
To hope that anyone wants to wait
Especially when I can't be sure
That a moment waits to hold my message,
Meaning my poem. I need your hope and your patience so
That you'll understand 'in the meantime' is now.